Guess What!

Student's Book 3A

Susannah Reed with Kay Bentley

Series Editor: Lesley Koustaff

CAMBRIDGE
UNIVERSITY PRESS

Contents

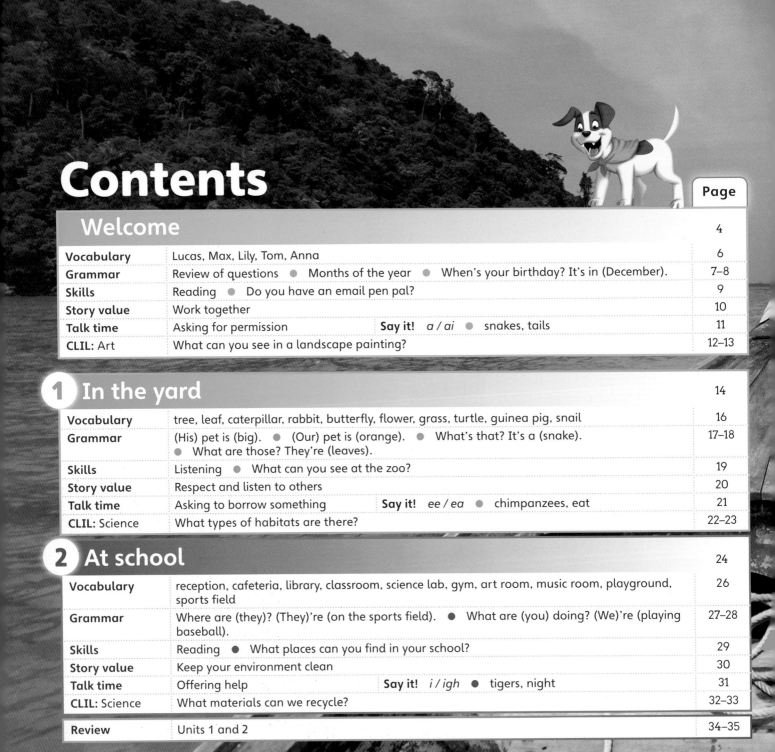

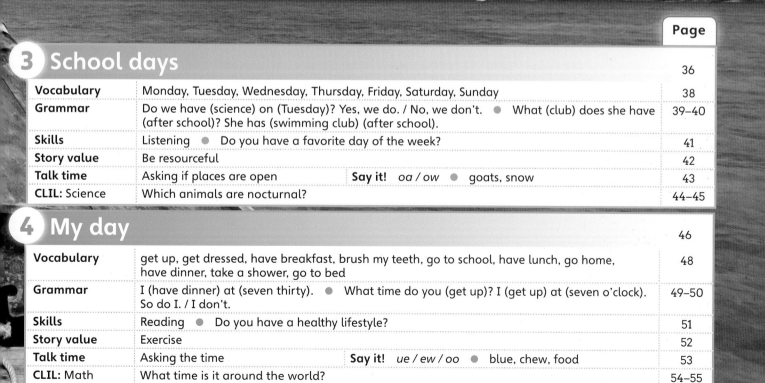

Welcome

Guess What!

5

1 ^{CD1 02} **Listen and point.**

2 ^{CD1 03} **Listen, point, and repeat.**

3 ^{CD1 04} **Listen and say the names.**

4 (Think) **Describe and guess who.**

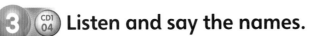

She's four years old.   Anna!

❶ Lucas
❷ Max
❸ Lily
❹ Tom
❺ Anna

5 (CD1 05) **Sing the song.**

Questions, questions,
I like asking questions.
What's your name?
How old are you?
What's your favorite color?

Questions, questions,
I like asking questions.
Do you like sports?
Do you have a pet?
Can you draw a picture of me?

Questions, questions,
I like asking questions.

Questions, questions ...

6 **Match the questions to the answers.**

1 What's your name?

2 How old are you?

3 What's your favorite color?

4 Do you like sports?

5 Do you have a pet?

6 Can you draw a picture of me?

a Yes, I do. I have a dog.

b I'm ten years old.

c Yes, I do. My favorite sports are swimming and tennis.

d Yes, I can. I like art.

e My name's Lily.

f My favorite color is yellow.

7 (About Me) **Ask and answer with a friend.**

What's your favorite color?

My favorite color is blue.

→ Workbook page 5

Grammar **7**

8 (CD1 06) **Listen and repeat.**

January

February

March

April

May

June

July

August

September

October

November

December

9 (CD1 07) **Listen and say the next month.**

January, February, March …   April!

10 (About Me) **Ask and answer with a friend.**

When's your birthday?   It's in June.

Remember!

When's your birthday?
It's in December.

11 (CD1 08) **Go to page 58. Listen and repeat the chant.**

→ Workbook page 6

Skills: *Reading and speaking*

 Let's start! **Do you have an email pen pal?**

12 (CD1 09) **Read and listen.**

Hi. My name's Juan. I'm ten years old. My birthday is in March.

I live in a small house with my family. I have two sisters and a brother. I don't have any pets, but I like animals.

I like basketball and field hockey, but my favorite sport is baseball. I like fishing, too.

What about you?

Email me back.

Juan

13 Read again and answer the questions.

1 How old is Juan?
2 When's his birthday?
3 How many brothers does he have?
4 Does he like animals?
5 Does he like sports?

14 (About Me) **Ask and answer with a friend.**

How old are you?
Do you have any brothers or sisters?
Do you have a pet?
What's your favorite sport?

Writing

 Workbook page 7: Write an email to a pen pal.

16 CD1 11 Talk Time **Listen and repeat. Then act.**

fly this kite   do this treasure hunt   go to the movie theater
play outside   go to the sports center

1

Can I play outside, please?

Yes, of course.

2

Can we go to the sports center, please?

No, I'm sorry, you can't.

Say it!

17 CD1 12 **Listen and repeat.**

Snakes make trails with their tails.

snake

What can you see in a landscape painting?

1 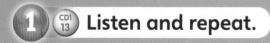 **Listen and repeat.**

1 river
2 ocean
3 waterfall
4 forest
5 mountain

2 **Watch the video.**

3 **What can you see in the landscape paintings?**

1

2

3

4

4 **What would you like to paint in a landscape painting?**

Guess What?

Chinese artists paint landscapes on rice paper and silk.

Project

5 **Make a fact file about a famous landscape artist.**

Name: Van Gogh
Paints: plants, forests
Country: France

1 In the yard

Guess What!

1 Listen and point.

2 Listen, point, and repeat.

3 Listen and say the words.

4 Think Describe and guess what.

It's a plant. It's green. Grass!

1. tree
2. leaf
3. caterpillar
4. rabbit
5. butterfly
6. flower
7. grass
8. turtle
9. guinea pig
10. snail

5 Sing the song.

My pet is white.
Your pet is gray.
Our pets aren't big,
They're small.
Where are our pets?
Can you see our pets?

Her pet is white.
His pet is gray.
Their pets aren't big,
They're small.
Where are their pets?
Can you see their pets?

6 Read and match. Then say the animal.

1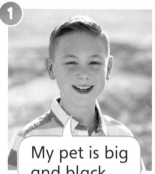
My pet is big and black.

2
Her pet is small and orange.

3
Our pet is small and yellow.

4
Their pet is gray and beautiful.

a

b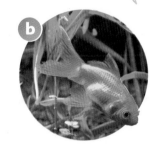

c

d

7 Look at the photographs. Ask and answer with a friend.

Number 3. Is their pet a bird?   Yes, it is.

Remember!

His pet is big.
Our pet is orange.

8 (CD1 18) **Listen and repeat.**

1
What's that?
It's a snail.

2
What are those?
They're butterflies.

9 (CD1 19) **Listen and say the numbers.**

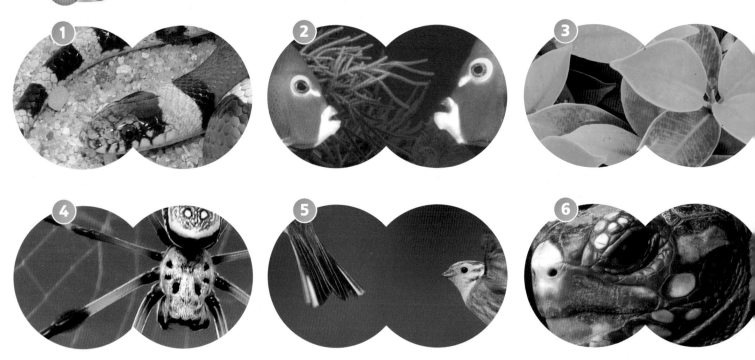

10 Look at the photographs.
Ask and answer with a friend.

11 (CD1 20) Go to page 58. Listen and repeat
the chant.

Remember!
What's that?
It's a snake.
What are those?
They're leaves.

Skills: *Listening and speaking*

Let's start! **What can you see at the zoo?**

12 CD1 21 **Listen and match.**

House of bugs

a

b

c

d

1 Lucy

2 Ryan

3 Sara

4 Jake

13 CD1 21 **Listen again and say *true* or *false*.**

1 Lucy likes snails.
2 Ryan likes ants.
3 Sara doesn't like the butterfly.
4 Jake doesn't like caterpillars.

14 (About Me) **Ask and answer with a friend.**

What is your favorite bug?
What color is it?
What bugs can you see outside?

Writing

➡ 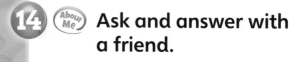 Workbook page 15: Write about your favorite bug.

15 CD1 22 **Read and listen.**

Value: Respect and listen to others

→ Workbook page 16

Listen and repeat. Then act.

computer game   toy car   eraser   camera   book

1

Can I borrow your camera, please?

Yes, you can.

2

Can I borrow your book, please?

No, I'm sorry, you can't.

Say it!

17 Listen and repeat.

Chimpanzees eat and sleep in trees.

chimpanzee

What types of **habitats** are there?

1 CD1 25 **Listen and repeat.**

1  desert

2  rain forest

3  grassland

4  tundra

2 Watch the video.

3 Match the habitats with the groups of animals.

1
monkey
crocodile
snake

2
lion
giraffe
snake

Guess What!

Deserts can be hot and cold. Antarctica is a desert.

desert
grassland
rain forest
tundra

3
spider
snake
camel

4
goat
sheep
bear

Project

5 Make a mind map for a habitat in your country.

4 What type of habitat would you like to visit?

→ Workbook page 18

CLIL: Science **23**

2 At school

Guess What!

1  Listen and point.

2 Listen, point, and repeat.

Welcome to Forest School

1. reception
2. cafeteria
3. library
4. classroom
5. science lab
6. gym
7. art room
8. music room
9. playground
10. sports field

3 Listen and say the places.

4 Think Describe and guess where.

This is Lily's favorite room.   Music room!

5 (CD1 29) Sing the song.

Dave and Daisy, where are you?
We're in the cafeteria.
Where are Dave and Daisy?
They're in the cafeteria.

Max and Mary, where are you?
We're in the music room.
Where are Max and Mary?
They're in the music room.

Sam and Susie, where are you?
We're on the sports field.
Where are Sam and Susie?
They're on the sports field.

6 Read and match.

1

2

3

a We're in the art room.

b We're on the playground.

c We're in the library.

7 Look at the pictures in activities 5 and 6. Ask and answer with a friend.

Where are they?

They're on the playground.

Remember!

Where are they?
They're **on the sports field.**

8 (CD1 30) **Listen and repeat.**

1
What are you doing?
We're playing tennis.

2
What are they doing?
They're playing tennis.

9 (CD1 31) **Look and find. Then listen and say the numbers.**

1 2 3 4 5

10 **Look at the picture. Ask and answer with a friend.**

What are they doing?

They're playing baseball.

Remember!
What **are** you doing?
We're play**ing** baseball.

11 (CD1 32) **Go to page 58. Listen and repeat the chant.**

Skills: *Reading and speaking*

Let's start! **What places can you find in your school?**

12 CD1 33 **Read and listen. Then match.**

1 My name's Lisa. Can you find a photograph of me? I'm standing outside my school. My school is big.

2 This is the playground. It's a big playground. Some children are playing a game of basketball. I like basketball, but my favorite sport is tennis.

3 This is a classroom. There's a board and some desks and chairs. These children are doing math. I like math, but my favorite class is art. I like drawing and painting.

4 This is my favorite room. It's our school library. There are lots of books, and I like reading. There are a lot of children in the library today.

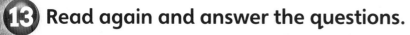

13 **Read again and answer the questions.**

1 Is Lisa's school big or small?
2 What is Lisa's favorite sport?
3 What are the children in the classroom doing?
4 Does Lisa like reading?

14 (About Me) **Make sentences about your school. Say *true* or *false*.**

Our school is small.   False. It's big.

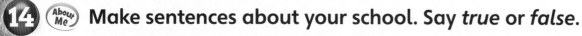

Writing

→ Workbook page 23: Write a description of your school.

15 CD1 34 **Read and listen.**

1 Look! It's your dad and Aunt Pat.

What are they doing?

They're picking up litter. Let's help.

SCHOOL FAIR TODAY

2 Hi, Aunt Pat. Can we help?

Yes, please. Can you pick up this litter?

Yes, of course.

3 Find a radio.

What a mess!

4 Where can we find a radio?

5 Come on, Lily!

Wait! Listen! What's that?

6 Look at this!

It's a radio!

Good job, Lily!

7 Thanks for your help! You can have the radio.

Thank you!

SCHOOL FAIR TODAY

Listen! This is my favorite song.

30 **Value:** Keep your environment clean

→ Workbook page 24

16   **Listen and repeat. Then act.**

pick up this litter   clean the living room   play nicely
put those toys in your room

Can I help you?

Yes. Can you clean the living room, please?

Yes, of course.

Thank you.

Say it!

17   **Listen and repeat.**

Tigers sometimes fight at night.

tigers

What materials can we recycle?

1 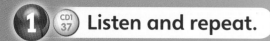 Listen and repeat.

recycling bin   paper   can   bottle   cardboard

2 Watch the video.

3 What can you recycle?

Guess What!

We can make recycled paper into paint.

Project

5 Make a colorful placemat from recycled cardboard.

4 What materials does your school recycle?

Review
Units 1 and 2

1 Find the months in the word puzzles.

Oct	ruary
Ju	ober
Feb	ember
Sept	ne

2  Listen and match the months to the photographs.

3 Look at each photograph. Answer the questions.

1 Where are they?
2 What are they doing?

4 Make your own word puzzles for your friend.

Choose months, nature, or places in school:
butter   rary
lib   fly

Carnival Day

Sports Day

Children's Day

Teacher's Day

→ Workbook pages 28–29

5 Play the game.

Start

What's that?　　It's a rabbit. Good. I have a rabbit.

What are those?　　They're spiders. I don't have spiders.

③ School days

Guess What!

1 **Listen and point.**

2 **Listen, point, and repeat.**

My week

My week ☺

3 **Listen and say the days.**

4 **Think** **Make sentences and guess the days.**

He has math, and she has science.

Monday!

❶ Monday
❷ Tuesday
❸ Wednesday
❹ Thursday
❺ Friday
❻ Saturday
❼ Sunday

5 (CD1 42) **Sing the song.**

We have math on Monday.
We don't have math on Tuesday.
Do we have math on Wednesday?
Yes, we do – on Wednesday, too.
We have math on Monday and Wednesday.

We have English on Thursday.
We don't have English on Friday.
Do we have English on Monday?
Yes, we do – on Monday, too.
We have English on Monday and Thursday.

6 **Make a schedule with a friend. Ask and answer.**

Do we have science on Monday?

No, we don't. We have science on Tuesday.

7 (About Me) **Make sentences about your schedule. Say *true* or *false*.**

We have music on Monday and Friday.

False!

We don't have music on Wednesday.

True!

Remember!
Do we have science on Tuesday?
Yes, we do.   No, we don't.

8 (CD1 43) **Listen and look. Then listen and repeat.**

Amy

in the morning   lunchtime   in the afternoon   dinnertime   after school

9 **Now read and answer the questions.**

1   What classes does Amy have in the morning?
2   What classes does Amy have in the afternoon?
3   What club does Amy have after school?
4   What class does Amy have before lunch?
5   What class does Amy have after lunch?

Amy has math and English in the morning.

10 (Think) **Choose a day from your schedule. Play a guessing game.**

What do you have in the morning?   I have math and science.

Is it Wednesday?   Yes, it is.

11 (CD1 44) **Go to page 58. Listen and repeat the chant.**

Remember!
What club does she have after school?
She has swimming club after school.

Skills: *Listening and speaking*

Let's start! **Do you have a favorite day of the week?**

12 (CD1 45) Listen and choose.

Caleb

Favorite day
Sunday

Morning
Swimming competition

Afternoon
Art club

Evening
Movie theater trip

Favorite day
Friday

Morning
Math test

Afternoon
Field trip to a farm

Evening
Field hockey club

Favorite day
Saturday

Morning
Art competition

Afternoon
Movie theater trip

Evening
Dance club

Maddie

Salima

13 (CD1 45) Listen again and say *true* or *false*.

1 Caleb's favorite class is math.
2 Salima's favorite class is music.
3 Maddie likes playing field hockey.
4 Salima likes dancing.

14 (About Me) Ask and answer with a friend.

What's your favorite class?
What clubs do you have after school?
Do you like competitions?
Do you like school tests?

Writing

→ **Workbook page 33: Write about your favorite day.**

15 CD1 46 **Read and listen.**

2

1 Find this painting.

What day is today?

It's Saturday.

Great! I like art. Let's go to the art gallery.

3 Is the art gallery open on Saturdays?

Yes, it is.

Come on. Let's go!

4 OK. Here we are.

Now where's the painting?

Over there!

5 What can we do now?

We can't take a photograph of the painting.

I have an idea!

6 Be careful!

Are you OK, Tom?

Yes, I'm fine. Don't worry.

7 It's very good, Tom.

What do you think, Max?

42   Value: Be resourceful

→ Workbook page 34

16 **Listen and repeat. Then act.**

art gallery   hospital   sports center   movie theater   library

1 Is the movie theater open on Sundays?

Yes, it is.

2 Is the library open on Mondays in the afternoon?

No, it isn't. It's closed.

Say it!

17 Listen and repeat.

goat

Goats need warm coats in the snow.

Which **animals** are nocturnal?

1 (CD1 49) **Listen and repeat.**

| 1 koala | 2 fox | 3 bat | 4 scorpion | 5 owl |

2 **Watch the video.**

3 **Which animals are nocturnal?**

Guess What!

At night, owls can see mice 18 m in front of them.

Project

5 Make a fact file about a nocturnal animal.

Animal: Koala
Country: Australia
Color: brown
Size: 70-90 cm
At night it eats food.
It can climb trees.

4 **Which animals in your country are nocturnal?**

4 My day

Guess What!

1 🔊 **Listen and point.**

2 🔊 **Listen, point, and repeat.**

❶ get up
❷ get dressed
❸ have breakfast
❹ brush my teeth
❺ go to school
❻ have lunch
❼ go home
❽ have dinner
❾ take a shower
❿ go to bed

3 🔊 **Listen and say the numbers.**

4 (Think) **Say the actions and guess the numbers.**

Go home.   Number 7!

5 (CD1 53) Sing the song.

I get up at 🕗 eight o'clock.
I have breakfast at 🕣 eight thirty.
I go to school at 🕘 nine o'clock,
And I have lunch at 🕧 twelve thirty.
Hey, hey, every day.

I go home at 🕞 three thirty,
And I play with my friends.
I have dinner at 🕢 seven thirty.
I go to bed at 🕘 nine o'clock at night.
Hey, hey, every day.

6 (CD1 54) Listen and say the names.

Emily

Sophie

Josh

Jacob

7 (About Me) Make sentences about your day. Say *true* or *false*.

I have breakfast at twelve thirty.

False!

> **Remember!**
> I have dinner at seven thirty.
> I go to bed at nine o'clock.

8 CD1 55 **Listen and repeat.**

What time do you have breakfast?

I have breakfast at eight o'clock.

So do I.

I don't. I have breakfast at seven thirty.

9 CD1 56 *About Me* **Listen and answer.**

10 *About Me* **Ask and answer with two friends.**

What time do you go to school?

I go to school at nine o'clock.

So do I.

I don't. I go to school at eight thirty.

Remember!

What time do you get up?
I get up **at seven o'clock**.
So do I.   I don't.

11 CD1 57 **Go to page 58. Listen and repeat the chant.**

Skills: *Reading and speaking*

 Do you have a healthy lifestyle?

12 (CD1 58) **Read and listen. Then answer the questionnaire.**

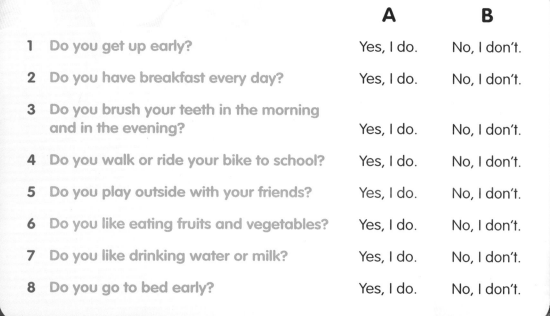

		A	B
1	Do you get up early?	Yes, I do.	No, I don't.
2	Do you have breakfast every day?	Yes, I do.	No, I don't.
3	Do you brush your teeth in the morning and in the evening?	Yes, I do.	No, I don't.
4	Do you walk or ride your bike to school?	Yes, I do.	No, I don't.
5	Do you play outside with your friends?	Yes, I do.	No, I don't.
6	Do you like eating fruits and vegetables?	Yes, I do.	No, I don't.
7	Do you like drinking water or milk?	Yes, I do.	No, I don't.
8	Do you go to bed early?	Yes, I do.	No, I don't.

Mostly As – Good job! You have a healthy lifestyle.
Mostly Bs – Hmm! What can you do to be more healthy?

13 **Now ask and answer with a friend.**

Do you get up early?   Yes, do. I get up at seven thirty.

Writing

 Workbook page 41: Write your own questionnaire.

→ Workbook page 42

15 CD1 60 **Listen and repeat. Then act.**

> five o'clock   four thirty   nine thirty   eight o'clock

Excuse me, what time is it, please?

It's eight o'clock.

Thank you.

Say it!

16 CD1 61 **Listen and repeat.**

Blue whales don't chew their food.

blue whales

What time is it around the world?

London 12:00

Dubai 15:00

Shanghai 19:00

Buenos Aires 08:00

1 CD1 62 Listen and repeat.

12:00
twelve o'clock

16:15
sixteen fifteen

10:30
ten thirty

23:45
twenty-three forty-five

2 Watch the video.

3 Match the pictures with the cities on page 54. What time is it?

4 What time is it in your country?

Guess What!

Brazil has three different time zones.

Project

5 Make a time chart of your day.

I get up at 7:00.
I eat lunch at 13:15.
I play tennis at 15:45.
I read my book in bed at 20:30.

Review

Units 3 and 4

1 Find the words in the puzzles and match to the photographs.

g* t* b*d

h*v* br**kf*st

pl*y t*nn*s

g* t* *rt cl*b

2 🎧 CD1 63 Listen and say the numbers.

3 Read Clara's sentences and say *true* or *false*.

1 I have eggs for breakfast.
2 I play soccer with my friends.
3 I have art club in the afternoon.
4 I go to bed at home.

4 Make your own word puzzles for your friend.

Choose days of the week or daily activities:
S*nd*y
T**sd*y

Clara

1

2

3

4

5 Play the game.

Yellow

What time do you (get up)?

I (get up) at (seven thirty).

Green

What do you have on (Monday) in the (morning)?

I have (English) at (nine o'clock).

Chants

Welcome (page 8)

 Listen and repeat the chant.

When's your birthday?
It's in June.
January, February, and March,
April, May, and June.

When's your birthday?
It's in December.
July, August, and September,
October, November, and December.

Unit 1 (page 18)

 Listen and repeat the chant.

What's that?
It's a snail.
What are those?
They're butterflies.

What's that?
It's a snake.
What are those?
They're leaves.

Unit 2 (page 28)

 Listen and repeat the chant.

What are you doing?
We're playing tennis.
What are they doing?
They're playing tennis.

What are you doing?
We're playing baseball.
What are they doing?
They're playing baseball.

Unit 3 (page 40)

 Listen and repeat the chant.

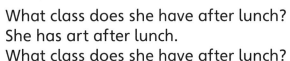

What class does she have after lunch?
She has art after lunch.
What class does she have after lunch?
She has art.

What club does she have after school?
She has swimming club after school.
What club does she have after school?
She has swimming club.

Unit 4 (page 50)

 Listen and repeat the chant.

What time do you have breakfast?
I have breakfast at eight o'clock.
So do I.
I don't.
I have breakfast at seven thirty.

What time do you go to school?
I go to school at nine o'clock.
So do I.
I don't.
I go to school at eight thirty.

Workbook 3A
with Online Resources

Contents

Lynne Marie Robertson

Series Editor: Lesley Koustaff

CAMBRIDGE
UNIVERSITY PRESS

Welcome

1 **Look and write the names.**

Anna   Lily   ~~Lucas~~   Max   Tom

1 _Lucas_
2 _____
3 _____
4 _____
5 _____

2 **Look at activity 1. Read and write _true_ or _false_.**

1   Tom likes art.   _true_

2   Anna is ten.   _____

3   Max is Lucas's dog.   _____

4   Lily's favorite sport is soccer.   _____

5   Lucas's favorite color is red.   _____

My picture dictionary **Go to page 48: Find and write the new words.**

4 Vocabulary

3 **Read and match.**

1 What's your name? ←   **a** I'm nine years old.
2 How old are you?   **b** My favorite color is green.
3 What's your favorite color? → **c** My name's Bill.
4 Do you like dogs?   **d** Yes, I can.
5 Do you have a bike?   **e** Yes, I do.
6 Can you ride a horse?   **f** No, I don't.

4 **Answer the questions. Then draw your picture.**

1 What's your name?

  My name is _____

2 How old are you?

  _____

3 Do you have a bike?

  _____

4 What's your favorite color?

  _____

  _____

5 Do you like dogs?

  _____

6 Can you play tennis?

  _____

Grammar **5**

5 (Think) **Write the months in order. Then answer the question. Use the letters in the boxes to complete the answer.**

1 J a n u a r y

2 F [ ] _ _ _ _ _ _ _

3 M _ _ _ _ _

4 A _ _ _ _ _

5 M _ _ _

6 J _ _ _[ ]

7 J _ _[ ]_ _

8 A _ _ _ _ _

9 S _ _ _ _ _ _ _ _

10 O _ [ ]_ _ _ _ _

11 N _ _[ ]_ _ _ _ _

12 D _ _ _ _ _ _ _

How many months are there?

_ _ W _ _ _ _ _

6 (About Me) **Answer the questions.**

1 What month is it?

It is _____

2 What's your favorite month?

_____

My picture dictionary → Go to page 48: Find and write the new words.

Skills: *Writing*

7 **Read the email. Circle the answers to the questions.**

Hello!
My name's Jill. I'm (eleven) years old. My birthday is in April.
I have one brother and one sister. I have a pet rabbit.
My favorite sport is basketball. What about you?
Jill ☺

1 How old are you?
2 When is your birthday?
3 Do you have any brothers or sisters?
4 Do you have a pet?
5 What's your favorite sport?

8 **(About Me) Look at activity 7. Answer the questions for you.**

1 *I'm* _____

2 _____

3 _____

4 _____

5 _____

9 **(About Me) Write an email to a pen pal.**

Hello! _____

My name's _____

_____

_____

_____

_____

10 **(About Me) Ask and answer with a friend.**

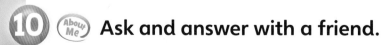

How old are you?   I'm eleven years old.

11 Read and number in order.

12 Look at activity 11. Write *yes* or *no*.

1 It's Tom's birthday.   *no*

2 The present is a cell phone.   _____

3 The treasure hunt is to find 7 things in 5 days.   _____

4 Lily's friends don't want to do the treasure hunt.   _____

5 The treasure hunt sounds fun.   _____

13 **Read and check the sentences that show the value: work together.**

1   Let's do the treasure hunt together.   ✓   2   Let's find my dog.   ☐

3   I like card games.   ☐   4   Good idea.   ☐

5   Let's clean up.   ☐   6   I'm playing basketball.   ☐

14 **Circle the words that sound like *snake*.**

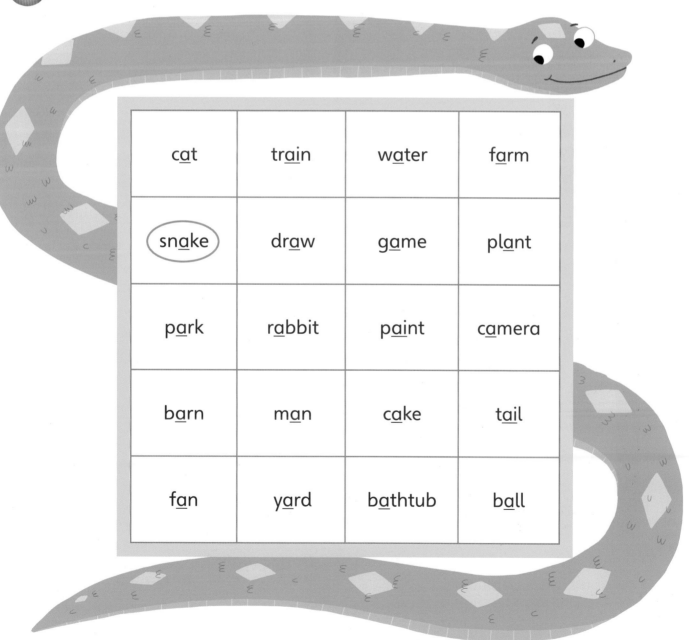

cat	train	water	farm
(snake)	draw	game	plant
park	rabbit	paint	camera
barn	man	cake	tail
fan	yard	bathtub	ball

What can you see in a landscape painting?

1 Look and match.

birds   boat   forest   mountain

plants   river   ocean   waterfall

2 Draw two landscapes.

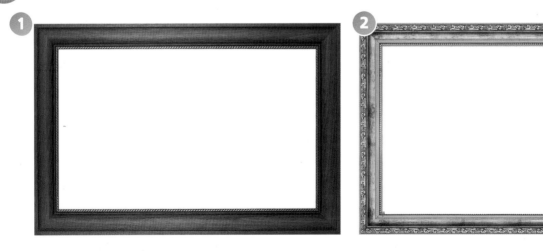

Draw a river.
Draw some trees behind it.
Draw a boat and three ducks on the river.

Draw four tall trees in a forest.
Draw some plants between the trees.
Draw an animal in the forest.

Evaluation

1 Do the word puzzle.

Down ↓

 ① ②

④

```
        1
        T
        O    4
    2  3 M
        
5
```

Across →

③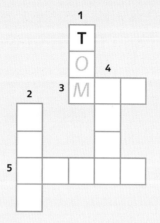

⑤

2 (About Me) Find and write the questions. Then answer.

1 are / old / you? / How

How old are you?

I'm

2 your / When's / birthday?

_____

_____

3 swim? / you / Can

_____

_____

4 color? / your / What's / favorite

_____

_____

5 you / Do / a / have / brother?

_____

_____

_____

3 (About Me) Complete the sentences about this unit.

1 I can talk about _____ .

2 I can write about _____ .

3 My favorite part is _____ .

4 (Puzzle) Guess what it is.

Go to page 53 and circle the answer.

11

1 In the yard

1 Look and guess. Then find and write the words.

 1 l l r i a r p a e c t

caterpillar

 2 t u b y t f l e r

_____

 3 s a g r s

_____

 4 r e l u t t

_____

 5 a i s l n

_____

 6 e a g i n u g i p

_____

 7 r e f w o l

_____

 8 e r e t

_____

 9 t r i b a b

_____

 10 f e l a

_____

2 Think Write the words from activity 1 on the lists.

Animals	Plants
caterpillar	*grass*
_____	_____
_____	_____
_____	_____
_____	

My picture dictionary → Go to page 49: Find and write the new words.

3 Look and circle the words.

1. My / *Your* pet is big.
2. His / Their pet is small.
3. His / Her pet is brown.
4. Our / My pet is beautiful.
5. My / Our pet is white.

4 Look and complete the sentences. Then color the animals.

~~Her~~ Her His Our   big big ~~small~~ small

1. *Her* pet is *small* and yellow.

2. _____ pet is _____ and gray.

3. _____ pet is _____ and brown.

4. _____ pet is _____ and orange.

5 Look and circle the questions and answers.

1 (What's that?)
   What are those?

a (It's a snail.)
   They're snails.

2 What's that?
   What are those?

b It's a flower.
   They're flowers.

3 What's that?
   What are those?

c It's a turtle.
   They're turtles.

4 What's that?
   What are those?

d It's a bird.
   They're birds.

5 What's that?
   What are those?

e It's a leaf.
   They're leaves.

6 Look and write the questions and answers.

butterflies   caterpillar   spider   trees

1 _What are those?_
   They're butterflies.
2 _What's that?_
   _____
3 _____
   _____
4 _____
   _____

Skills: *Writing*

7 Read the paragraph and write the words.

> butterflies   leaves   ~~small~~   tree   white

My favorite bug is a caterpillar. Caterpillars are ¹ *small* . I like black
and ² _____ caterpillars. You can see a caterpillar on a ³ _____ .
The caterpillar eats the green ⁴ _____ . Beautiful ⁵ _____ come
from caterpillars.

8 (About Me) Answer the questions.

1 What's your favorite bug?
My favorite bug is _____

2 What color is it?
_____

3 Is it big or small or beautiful?
_____

4 Where can you see it?
_____

9 (About Me) Write about your favorite bug.

My favorite bug _____
_____
_____
_____
_____
_____

10 (About Me) Ask and answer with a friend.

What's your favorite animal?   My favorite animal is a horse.

11 Read and match.

1 Not now, Anna.	**2** Sorry, Anna. Thank you.
3 Are those ears and a tail?	**4** Can we borrow it, please?

12 Look at activity 11. Answer the questions.

1 What do they see behind the tree?   *Ears and a tail.*

2 What animal is behind the tree?   _____

3 What animal does Anna have?   _____

4 What can they do with it?   _____

5 Who is sorry?   _____

13 Look and write the questions and answers. Then check the picture that shows the value: respect and listen to others.

> ~~Can I help?~~   Yes, you can. Thank you.   Can I help?   Not now.

1 Can I help?

2

14 Write the words with the same sound in the lists.

> ~~cake~~   ~~tree~~   p**ai**nt   l**ea**f   m**a**ke   j**ea**ns
> sl**ee**p   **ea**t   t**ai**l   chimpanz**ee**   tr**ai**n   sn**a**ke

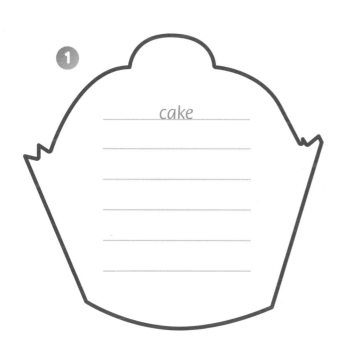

1

cake

2

tree

What types of habitats are there?

1 **Write the names of the habitats. Then circle the two correct sentences.**

desert   grassland   ~~rain forest~~   tundra

rain forest

It's a hot place.
There are a lot of trees and leaves.
Lions live here.

_____

It's a cold place.
There are lots of trees.
Bears live here.

It's a hot place.
Monkeys live here.
There is a lot of grass.

_____

There is little water.
Snakes and spiders live here.
There are lots of fish.

2 **Draw and write about a habitat in your country.**

It's a _____ place. There are lots of _____ . _____ live here.

Evaluation

1 **Find and write the words.**

1 <u>What's that?</u>
It's a flower.

2 _____
They're leaves.

3 _____
They're caterpillars.

4 _____
It's a butterfly.

5 _____
It's grass.

2 (Think) **Look and write the words.**

| ~~My~~ Your Our Their | ~~turtle~~ fish rabbit snail | ~~small~~ big white green |

<u>   My   </u> <u>   turtle   </u>   _____   _____   _____

is <u>   small   </u> .   is _____ .   is _____ .   is _____ .

3 (About Me) **Complete the sentences about this unit.**

1 I can talk about _____ .

2 I can write about _____ .

3 My favorite part is _____ .

4 (Puzzle) **Guess what it is.**

Go to page 53 and circle the answer.

2 At school

1 Look and number the picture.

1 playground
2 gym
3 science lab
4 sports field
5 cafeteria
6 art room
7 library
8 music room
9 reception
10 classroom

2 (Think) Look at activity 1. Read the sentences and write the words.

1 You can paint pictures in this room   *art room*

2 There are desks and chairs in this room. _____

3 You can eat lunch in this room. _____

4 You have a science class in this room. _____

5 You can run, jump, and dance in this room. _____

6 You go here when you visit the school. _____

7 You can play soccer here. _____

8 You can play outside here. _____

9 You can read books here. _____

10 You can sing here. _____

My picture dictionary ➔ Go to page 50: Find and write the new words.

3 Look and circle the answers.

We're / (They're) on the sports field.

We're / They're in the art room.

We're / They're in the science lab.

We're / They're in the classroom.

4 Think Look and complete the questions and answers.

We're in the library!

Hello!

Hi!

1 Where are ___they___ ?   _____ at reception.

2 Where are _____ ?   ___We're___ in the library.

3 Where are _____ ?   _____ in the gym.

4 Where are _____ ?   _____ in the music room.

5 Where are _____ ?   _____ on the playground.

5 Read and match.

a They're playing basketball.

b They're playing soccer.

c We're playing basketball.

d We're playing soccer.

6 (Think) Look and write the questions and answers.

1 <u>What are you doing?</u>   <u>We're playing ice hockey.</u>

2 <u>What are they doing?</u>   <u>They're</u>

3 _____   _____

4 _____   _____

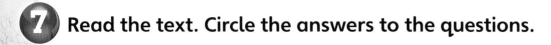

Skills: *Writing*

7 **Read the text. Circle the answers to the questions.**

My school is (small.) There are six classrooms, a library, and a big playground.

I like the library, but my favorite room is the gym. There are 18 children in my

classroom. My favorite class is English.

1 Is your school big or small?
2 What rooms and places are in your school?
3 What is your favorite room?
4 How many children are in your class?
5 What is your favorite class?

8 (About Me) **Look at activity 7. Answer the questions.**

1 *My school is* _____

2 _____

3 _____

4 _____

5 _____

9 **Write a description of your school.**

My school _____

_____

_____

_____

_____

_____

_____

10 (About Me) **Ask and answer with a friend.**

What's your favorite class?   My favorite class is science.

11 Read and write the words.

> Thank you!   pick up   ~~litter~~   Listen!

a

What are they doing?

They're picking up _litter_ . Let's help.

b

Hi, Aunt Pat. Can we help?

Yes, please. Can you _____ this litter?

c

Come on, Lily!

Wait! _____ What's that?

d

Thanks for your help! You can have the radio.

12 Look at activity 11. Write *yes* or *no*.

1 Dad and Aunt Pat are in the gym.   _no_

2 Aunt Pat is picking up litter.   ____

3 The children don't help.   ____

4 Lily is listening to the radio.   ____

5 Aunt Pat wants the radio.   ____

13 Look and check the pictures that show the value: keep your environment clean.

14 Circle the words that sound like *tiger*.

What materials can we recycle?

1 **Look and match.**

2 **Design two recycling bins for your school.**

Where is it? _____

_____

What can children put in it? _____

_____

Where is it? _____

_____

What can children put in it? _____

_____

Evaluation

 Look and answer the questions.

1 Where are the girls? *They're in the gym.*

2 What are they doing? _____

3 Where are the boys? _____

4 What are they doing? _____

5 Where are the teachers? _____

6 What are they doing? _____

7 Where are we? _____

8 What are we doing? _____

  Complete the sentences about this unit.

1 I can talk about _____ .

2 I can write about _____ .

3 My favorite part is _____ .

 Guess what it is.

Go to page 53 and circle the answer.

Review Units 1 and 2

1 Look and find the numbers. Answer the questions.

1 Where are they? _They're in the science lab._

2 What are those? _____

3 What's he doing? _____

4 What are those? _____

5 What are they doing? _____

6 Where are they? _____

7 What's that? _____

8 What's that? _____

2 Think Find 11 months ↓ →. Then answer the question.

```
N O V E M B E R T J S F G M
A C B Z A P Y E J U N E K A
W T A Q Y N A C I L T B O R
B O N (J A N U A R Y) S R I C
K B U P B T A N G K W U L H
D E C E M B E R X A C A G M
O R O C G M A I O A P R I L
P B Y A U G U S T W B Y J D
```

One month is not in the puzzle. What month is it?

_____

3 Look and write the questions.

1 *What's her name?*   It's Kate.
2 _____ It's in May.
3 _____ Her favorite color is pink.
4 *Who are they?*   They're my cousins.
5 _____ They're at the park.
6 _____ They're flying a kite.

4 Look at the photographs in Activity 3. Complete the sentences.

1 _____ *His T-shirt* _____ is yellow.   2 _____ is pink.
3 _____ are blue.   4 _____ is a plane.

5 Think Answer the questions.

> a bird   a butterfly   a caterpillar   a cafeteria
> February   grass   ~~a guinea pig~~   a library

1 These eat leaves. What are they? ___ *a guinea pig* ___ and _____
2 You can eat here. Where is it? _____
3 You can read books here. Where is it? _____
4 These can fly. What are they? _____ and _____
5 This has 8 letters. What month is it? _____
6 This is a plant. What is it? _____

School days

1 Write the days of the week.

	n a d y M o _Monday_	a u s d e T y	s d a y d e n W e
Sue			
Dan			

Dan   Sue

	y h r d u T s a	i a y F d r	y r t d S a a u	y S n d u a
Sue				
Dan				

2 Look at activity 1. Write yes or no.

1 She has math on Thursday. _____ _yes_

2 He has gym on Friday. _____

3 She has art on Monday. _____

4 He has soccer club on Saturday. _____

5 She has computer club on Sunday. _____

3 Look at activity 1. Write the sentences.

1 Monday: _She has music, and he has science._

2 Tuesday: _____

3 Wednesday: _____

4 Thursday: _____

5 Friday: _____

My picture dictionary **Go to page 51: Find and write the new words.**

4 Think Look and follow. Then complete the questions and answers.

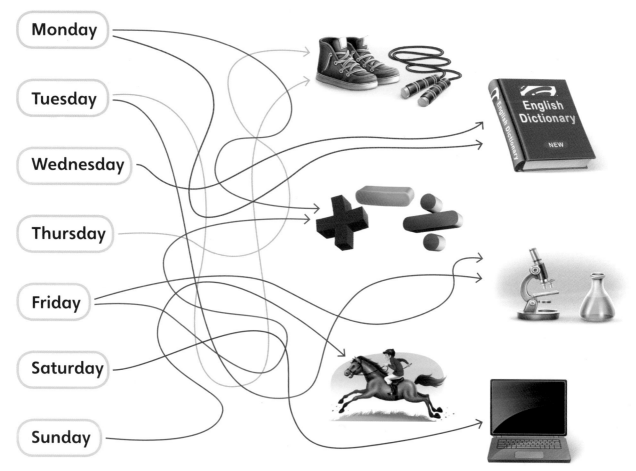

Monday

Tuesday

Wednesday

Thursday

Friday

Saturday

Sunday

1   Do we have gym on Thursday?   *Yes, we do.*

2   Do we have English on Saturday?   _____

3   Do we have math on Monday?   _____

4   _____ science on Friday?   _____

5   _____ computer club on Sunday?   _____

6   _____ horseback riding club on Sunday?   _____

5 Look at activity 4. Complete the sentences.

1   *We don't have*   math on Thursday.

2   _____   English on Monday and Wednesday.

3   _____   science on Tuesday and Friday.

4   _____   horseback riding club on Thursday.

5   _____   computer club on Saturday.

6   _____   gym on Monday and Friday.

Read and complete Josh's day.

Monica
Which classes do you have on Tuesday?

Josh
We have gym, science, and art in
the morning. Gym is before science.
Art is after science.

Monica
Which classes do you have in the afternoon?

Josh
We have English and math. We have English
after lunch. We have math after English.

Monica
Do you have a club after school?

Josh
Yes, I have soccer club in the evening.

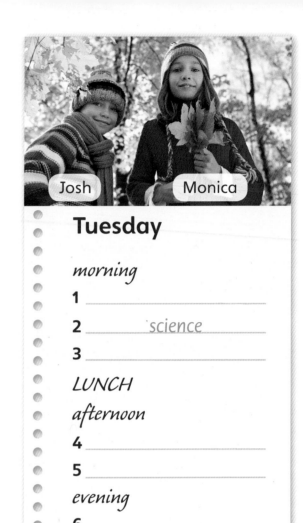

Josh   Monica

Tuesday

morning
1 _____
2 _____ *science*
3 _____

LUNCH
afternoon
4 _____
5 _____
evening
6 _____

7 Look at activity 6. Write the answers.

1 Which class does Josh have after gym?

   He has science after gym.

2 Which class does Josh have after lunch?

   _____

3 Which class does Josh have before lunch?

   _____

4 Which class does Josh have before math?

   _____

8 **Choose a day from your schedule. Answer the questions.**

1 Which classes do you have in the morning?

   _____

2 Which classes do you have in the afternoon?

   _____

3 Do you have a club after school?

   _____

Skills: *Writing*

9 **Read the paragraph and write the words.**

> horseback   club   morning   ~~Saturday~~   music   competitions

My favorite day of the week is ¹ _Saturday_ . I have a ² _____

class in the ³ _____ . I have photography ⁴ _____ in the afternoon.

In the evening. I have a ⁵ _____ riding lesson and a dance

competition. I like ⁶ _____ .

10 (About Me) **Answer the questions.**

1 What's your favorite day of the week?

   My favorite day is _____

2 What do you have in the morning?

   _____

3 What do you have in the afternoon?

   _____

4 What do you have in the evening?

   _____

11 (About Me) **Write about your favorite day.**

My favorite _____

_____

_____

_____

_____

_____

12 (About Me) **Ask and answer with a friend.**

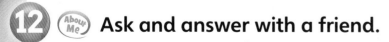

Do you have any clubs this week?

Yes, I have computer club on Thursday.

13 Read and number in order.

a
It's very good, Tom.
What do you think, Max?

b
We can't take a photograph of the painting.
What can we do now?
I have an idea!

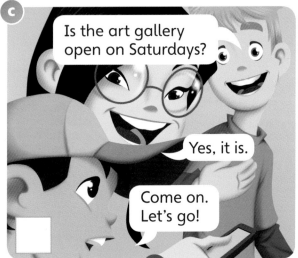

c
Is the art gallery open on Saturdays?
Yes, it is.
Come on. Let's go!

d
Be careful!
Are you OK, Tom?
Yes, I'm fine. Don't worry.

e
OK. Here we are.
Now where's the painting?
Over there!

f
What day is it today?
Find this painting.
It's Saturday.
1
Great! I like art. Let's go to the art gallery.

14 Look at activity 13. Answer the questions.

1 Who likes art? _Tom._

2 What is open on Saturdays? _____

3 What can't they do? _____

4 What animal is in the painting? _____

5 What does Tom do? _____

15 Look and check the pictures that show the value: be resourceful.

16 Color the words that sound like *goat*. Then answer the question.

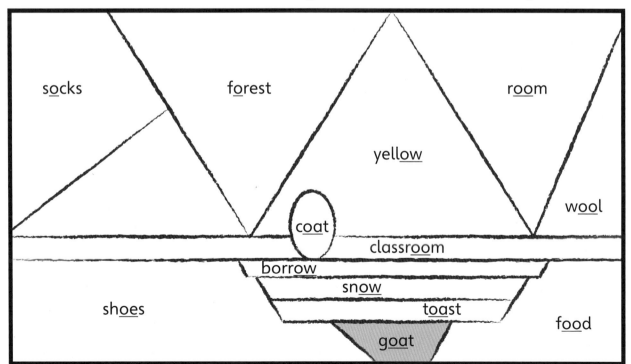

socks   forest   room

yellow

wool

coat

classroom

borrow

snow

toast

shoes   goat   food

What's in the picture? _____

Which animals are nocturnal?

1 **Read and check the sentences that are true for nocturnal animals.**

1 It finds food and eats at night. ☑

2 It likes running and flying in the day. ☐

3 It likes playing in the evening and at night. ☐

4 It sleeps in the morning and afternoon. ☐

2 **Draw and label one animal in each box in the chart.**
Then write sentences about each animal.

	✓ nocturnal	✗ nocturnal
✗ fly	**1**	**2**
✓ fly	**3**	**4**

1 *A scorpion is nocturnal. It can't fly.*

2 _____

3 _____

4 _____

Evaluation

Emily   Jacob

1 Write the days of the week in the diary and answer the questions.

T_hursday_		Sa_____	
10:00	art	3:00	gym competition
2:00	English test		
6:00	soccer club		
F_____		S_____	
9:00	gym	10:00	photography club
1:00	science	12:00	lunch with Grandma

1 Do you have art on Friday?   _No, we don't._

2 Do you have art on Thursday?   _____

3 Do you have a math test on Thursday?   _____

4 Do you have a gym competition on Saturday?   _____

2 **Look at activity 1. Answer the questions about Emily.**

1 Look at Thursday. What does she have in the morning?   _She has art._

2 Look at Thursday. What does she have in the evening?   _____

3 Look at Friday. What does she have in the morning?   _____

4 Look at Friday. What does she have in the afternoon?   _____

5 Look at Sunday. What does she have before lunch?   _____

3 **Complete the sentences about this unit.**

1 I can talk about _____ .

2 I can write about _____ .

3 My favorite part is _____ .

4 Puzzle **Guess what it is.**

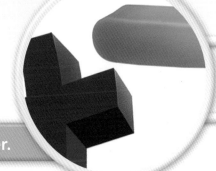

Go to page 53 and circle the answer.

My day

1 Look and write the answers.

> brush your teeth   get up   go to bed   ~~go to school~~
> have breakfast   have dinner   have lunch   take a shower

 go to school

 _____

 _____

 _____

 _____

 _____

 _____

 _____

2 (About Me) Look at activity 1. Write six sentences about your day.

1 I ____get dressed____ in the morning.

2 I _____

3 I _____ in the afternoon.

4 I _____ in the evening.

5 _____

6 _____

My picture dictionary Go to page 52: Find and write the new words.

3 Read and match.

1 I get dressed at seven o'clock.

2 I go to school at eight o'clock.

3 I eat lunch at twelve o'clock.

4 I go home at three thirty.

5 I eat dinner at seven thirty.

6 I go to bed at nine thirty.

4 Look and complete the sentences.

1 I _____get up_____ at _____seven thirty_____ .

2 I _____ at _____ .

3 I _____ at _____ .

4 I _____ at _____ .

5 I _____ at _____ .

6 I _____ at _____ .

5 (About Me) Write sentences and draw the times.

1 I _____ at _____ .

2 I _____ at _____ .

3 I _____ at _____ .

4 I _____ at _____ .

6 (Think) **Read and answer the questions.**

Ken: What time do you get up?
Eva: I get up at seven thirty.
Ken: So do I.
Maya: I don't. I get up at seven o'clock.
Maya: What time do you go to bed?
Ken: I go to bed at nine o'clock.
Eva: I don't. I go to bed at eight thirty.
Maya: So do I.

Maya   Eva   Ken

1   Who gets up at seven o'clock?   *Maya*
2   Who gets up at seven thirty?   _____ and _____
3   Who goes to bed at eight thirty?   _____ and _____
4   Who goes to bed at nine o'clock?   _____

7 **Look and complete the sentences.**

1   What time do you have dinner?

     I ___*have dinner*___ at ___*seven o'clock*___ .

     So do I.   I don't.

2   What time do you have breakfast?

     I _____ at _____ .

     I _____ at _____ .   _____

8 (About Me) **Ask and answer with two friends.**

I get up at …   So do I.   I don't. I get up at …

Skills: *Writing*

9 **Write a questionnaire about a healthy lifestyle. Then ask a friend.**

~~have breakfast~~   play outside   ~~walk to school~~   ride a bike
~~get up~~   brush your teeth   watch TV   play sports
play computer games   drink orange juice

Yes / No

1 Do you have breakfast every day? _____ _____

2 Do you walk to school in the morning? _____ _____

3 Do you like getting up early? _____ _____

4 _____ _____

5 _____ _____

6 _____ _____

7 _____ _____

8 _____ _____

9 _____ _____

10 _____ _____

10 **Ask and answer with a friend.**

Do you have a healthy lifestyle?   Yes, I do. I walk to school every day.

11 Read and match.

1 I can do the race!
2 Thanks! Swimming is fun!
3 The first prize is a watch!
4 And the winner is … Lucas!

Find a watch.

SWIMMING

Look! A swimming race!

3

Yes, good idea!

Hooray!

Good job, Lucas!

12 Look at activity 11. Circle the answers.

1 Lucas does _____ .
   a a swimming club   b a swimming race   c the first prize

2 Lucas thinks swimming is _____ .
   a fun   b great   c nice

3 Lucas wins _____ .
   a a present   b a test   c a prize

4 The prize is _____ .
   a a watch   b a race   c swimming lessons

Check the activities that show the value: exercise.

1	do a bike race	✓	2	go to baseball club	
3	take a math test		4	play in a tennis competition	
5	go to bed early		6	go roller-skating	
7	take a shower		8	play sports after school	

 Circle the words that sound like *blue*.

START!

blue	equals	snow	jump	toast	sausage
turn	June	run	goat	excuse	plus
yellow	mouth	shoots	chew	duck	room

FINISH!

What time is it around the world?

1 **Look and answer the questions.**

1 What time is it in Buenos Aires?

It's ___eight o'clock___ in the morning.

2 What time is it in London?

It's _____ in the afternoon.

3 What time is it in Dubai?

It's _____ .

4 What time is it in Shanghai?

It's _____ .

2 **Draw a picture and write sentences.**

1 I _____ at eight o'clock in the morning.

2 I _____
_____ .

3 I _____
_____ .

4 I _____
_____ .

Evaluation

1 Look and complete the questions and answers.

1 **What time do you get up?**

I get up at six thirty.

2 **What time do you get dressed?**

_____

3 _____

I go to school at eight o'clock.

4 _____

I have dinner at seven thirty.

5 **What time do you brush your teeth?**

_____

6 _____

I go to bed at nine o'clock.

2 Look at activity 1. Write sentences. Start with *So do I* or *I don't*.

1 *So do I. I get up at six thirty.* _____

2 _____

3 _____

4 _____

5 _____

6 _____

3 Complete the sentences about this unit.

1 I can talk about _____ .

2 I can write about _____ .

3 My favorite part is _____ .

4 Puzzle Guess what it is.

Go to page 53 and circle the answer.

Review Units 3 and 4

1 Look and complete the sentences about my day.

> after lunch   after school   at four o'clock
> at nine o'clock.   at six thirty   at ten o'clock

 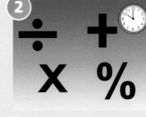 

1 I go to school _at nine o'clock_ .   2 We have math _____ .

3 We have art _____ .   4 We have tennis club _____ .

5 I go home _____ .   6 I have dinner _____ .

2 (About Me) Write questions and answers.

get up   go to bed   have breakfast | on Monday   on Saturday   on Sunday

1 _What time do you get up on Monday?_ _____

   I get up _____

2 _____

   _____

3 _____

   _____

3 **Find the words ↓ →. Use the words to complete the verbs.**

1

get _dressed_

```
B H F D T E E T H
R W V I P K E X M
E L U N C H L U S
A O Y N C G B A C
K D R E S S E D H
F M E R B O D C O
A Z R W E G H H O
S H O W E R Q R L
T X L B A U P C Z
```

2

take a _____

3

brush your _____

4

have _____

5

go to _____

6

have _____

7

have _____

8

go to _____

4 **Answer the questions.**

1 What day starts with the letter *M*? _____ _Monday_

2 What day has nine letters? _____

3 What day comes after Thursday? _____

4 What day comes before Sunday? _____

5 What day has the letter *H* in it? _____

6 What day sounds like M<u>o</u>nday? _____

7 Put these letters in order: YADSUTE. _____

Welcome

Lucas   Anna   Max   Tom   Lily

March   December   January   August   April   October
June   November   May   February   July   September

J _ _ _ _ _ _ _	F _ _ _ _ _ _ _	M _ _ _ _
A _ _ _ _	M _ _	J _ _ _
J _ _ _	A _ _ _ _	S _ _ _ _ _ _ _
O _ _ _ _ _	N _ _ _ _ _ _	D _ _ _ _ _ _

1 In the yard

snail   guinea pig   caterpillar   turtle   butterfly
tree   flower   grass   rabbit   leaf

2 At school

reception   library   sports field   classroom   gym   music room
cafeteria   art room   playground   science lab

3 School days

Saturday   Tuesday   Monday   Thursday
Sunday   Wednesday   Friday

M _ _ _ _ _ _ _

T _ _ _ _ _ _ _

W _ _ _ _ _ _ _

T _ _ _ _ _ _ _

F _ _ _ _ _

S _ _ _ _ _ _

S _ _ _ _ _

4 My day

go to school   get up   take a shower   have breakfast   get dressed

have lunch   go home   have dinner   brush your teeth   go to bed

1 **Find the words ↓ →. Use the colored letters to answer the question.**

P	G	L	I	B	R	A	R	Y	A	R	C	U	B
I	Q	E	R	T	G	Y	J	K	E	L	P	V	E
N	L	A	B	U	T	T	E	R	F	L	Y	U	V
E	B	Z	M	S	W	L	H	B	G	T	D	A	M
A	M	N	F	O	T	D	W	B	I	I	S	O	A
P	G	O	A	O	S	H	O	W	E	R	H	X	T
P	A	A	N	M	G	I	R	C	M	Q	E	Z	H
L	S	G	N	H	K	L	U	Y	O	O	L	P	M
E	M	U	A	N	T	U	E	R	N	S	L	L	Y
X	V	I	E	B	G	H	Y	O	P	W	F	R	Y
D	O	T	H	E	D	I	S	H	E	S	O	K	R
J	K	A	S	K	V	B	Y	U	W	E	T	R	E
M	I	R	W	T	E	C	J	F	H	A	N	N	A

Q: What are two things people can't eat before breakfast?

A: _ _ _ _ _ _   and   _ _ _ _ _ _

Story fun

1 **Match the objects to the words. Then match the words to the story units they come from.**

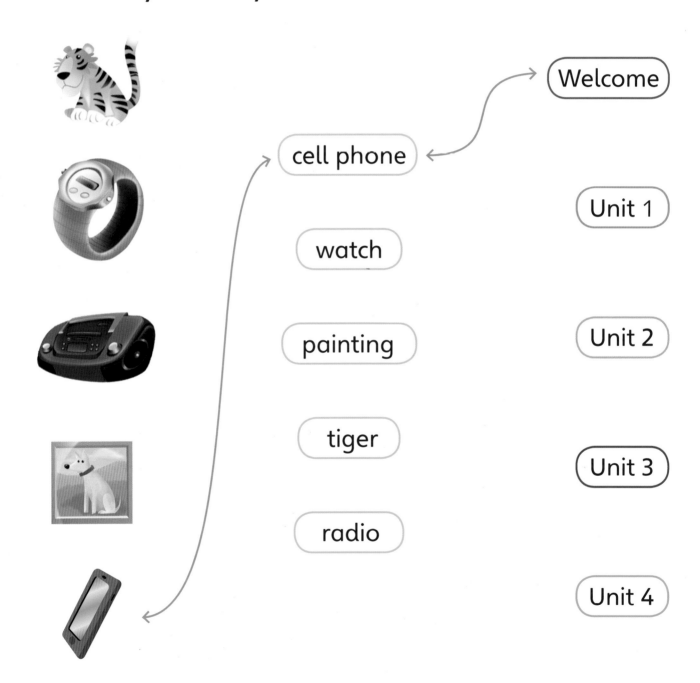

Welcome

cell phone

watch

Unit 1

painting

Unit 2

tiger

Unit 3

radio

Unit 4

1 Write the numbers in the box of the objects.

1
2
3
4
5

Thanks and Acknowledgements

Many thanks to everyone in the excellent team at Cambridge University Press. In particular we would like to thank Emily Hird, Liane Grainger, and Melissa Bryant whose professionalism, enthusiasm, experience, and talent makes them all such a pleasure to work with.

We would also like to give special thanks to Lesley Koustaff for her unfailing support, expert guidance, good humor, and welcome encouragement throughout the project.

The authors and publishers would like to thank the following contributors:
Blooberry Design: concept design, cover design, book design, page makeup
Charlotte Aldis: editorial training
Fiona Davis: editing
Lisa Hutchins: freelance editing
Ann Thomson: art direction, picture research
Gareth Boden Photography: commissioned photography
Ian Harker: audio recording
James Richardson: song and chant composition, arrangement of theme tune
Vince Cross: theme tune composition
John Marshall Media: audio recording and production
Phaebus: video production
hyphen S.A.: publishing management, American English edition

The authors and publishers acknowledge the following sources of copyright material and are grateful for the permissions granted. Although every effort has been made, it has not always been possible to identify the sources of all the material used, or to trace all copyright holders. If any omissions are brought to our notice, we will be happy to include the appropriate acknowledgments on reprinting.

The authors and publishers would like to thank the following illustrators:

Student's Book
Pablo Gallego: pp. 5, 6, 10, 15, 16, 20, 25, 26, 30, 37, 38, 42, 47, 48, 52; Luke Newell: pp. 7, 17, 27, 39, 49; A Corazon Abierto: pp. 28; Marcus Cutler: pp. 35, 57; Mark Duffin: p. 54.

Workbook
Pablo Gallego (Beehive Illustration): pp. 3, 4, 8, 11, 16, 24, 34, 42, 48; Gareth Conway (Bright Agency): pp. 9, 14, 38; Brian Lee: pp. 10, 18; Humberto Blanco (Sylvie Poggio): pp. 13, 21, 27, 45; Simon Walmesley: pp. 13, 14, 22, 28, 39; A Corazon Abierto (Sylvie Poggio): p. 17; Ilias Arahovitis (Beehive Illustration): pp. 19, 20, 26, 30, 31, 37; Luke Newell: pp. 19, 35; Marcus Cutler (Sylvie Poggio): pp. 25, 35; Graham Kennedy: pp. 29, 36, 46; Mark Duffin: pp. 22, 44; Monkey Feet: pp. 49, 50, 52.

The authors and publishers would like to thank the following for permission to reproduce photographs:

Student's Book
p.2-3: serhi000111/Shutterstock; p.4-5: TongRo Images/Alamy; p.8: Kali9/Getty Images; p.9 (B/G): KPG_Payless/Shutterstock, (TR): OJO Images Ltd/Alamy, (BL): Herve GYSSELS/Photononstop/Corbis; p. 11 (B/G) & p.43 (B/G): Robert Harding Picture Library Ltd/Alamy); p.11 (BR): Paul Chesley/Getty Images; p.12: Martyn Goddard/Alamy; p.13 (1)T: Jaroslaw Grudzinski/Shutterstock, (2)T: Galyna Andrushko/Shutterstock, (3)T: Nicha/Shutterstock, (4)T: konzeptm/Shutterstock, (5)T: Calin Tatu/Shutterstock, (1)B: iBird/Shutterstock, (2)B: nodff/Shutterstock, (3)B: antpkr/Shutterstock, (4)B: Lillya Kulianionak/Shutterstock, (Van Gogh)BR project: Chris Hellier/Alamy, (Van Gogh painting) BR project: World History Archive/Alamy; p.14-15: David Wong/Getty Images; p.17 (a): crazychris84/Shutterstock, (b): S-F/Shutterstock, (c): ARTSILENSE/Shutterstock, (d): Ivan Cholakov/Shutterstock, p.18 (TL): NREY/Shutterstock, (R): Michael Warwick/Shutterstock, (1): Matt Jeppson/Shutterstock, (2): Carlos Villoch-MagicSea.com/Alamy, (3): jajaladdawan/Shutterstock, (4): FloridaStock/Shutterstock, (5): Ernie James/Alamy, (6): reptiles4all/Shutterstock; p.19 (B/G): liubomir/Shutterstock, (a): Ryan M. Bolton/Shutterstock, (b): Purestock/Alamy, (c): James Laurie/Shutterstock, (d): Toshe Ognjanov/Shutterstock, (1) & (2) & p.56 (3): Monkey Business Images/Shutterstock, (3): Liudmila P. Sundikova/Shutterstock, (4): Brocreative/Shutterstock; p.21 (B/G): szefei/iStockphoto; p.21 (B): Suzi Eszterhas/Minden Pictures/FLPA; p.22: Laszlo Halasi/Shutterstock; p.23 (1): Fabio Pupin/FLPA, (2): Luciano Candisani/Minden Pictures/Corbis, (3): Frans Lanting/FLPA, (4): Carole-Anne Fooks/Alamy; p.24-25: Kike Calvo/National Geographic Society/Corbis; p.29 (B/G): Mark Herreid/Shutterstock, (a): Michael DeLion/Getty Images, (b): Gabe Palmer/Alamy, (c): Hero Images/Corbis, (d): Antenna/fstop/Corbis; p.31(B/G): David Cayless/Getty Images; p.31 (BR): fStop/Alamy; p.32 & p.33 (5): Lightspring/Shutterstock; p.33 (1)T: Marquisphoto/Shutterstock, (2)T: Ulrich Mueller/Shutterstock, (3)T: italianestro/Shutterstock, (4)T: pixinoo/Shutterstock, (1)B: aurenar/Shutterstock, (2)B: Janie Airey/Getty Images, (3)B: Jupiterimages/Getty Images, (4)B: Brand X Pictures/Getty Images; p.34 (CB): Ambient Images Inc/Alamy, (CT): Sally & Richard Greenhill/Alamy, (T): criben/Shutterstock, (B): JLP/Jose L. Pelaez/Corbis; p.36-37: Randy Plett/Getty Images; p. 40 (TR): Christine Langer-Pueschel/Shutterstock, (TL): Trevor Smith/Alamy, (BL): igor kisselev/Shutterstock, (TC): Image Source/Alamy; p.40 (BC): Ian Lishman/Juice Images/Corbis, (BR): VIEW Pictures Ltd/Alamy, p.41 (B/G): ThomasLENNE/Shutterstock, (CL): sianc/Shutterstock, (CR): PT Images/Shutterstock, (BL): D. Hurst/Alamy; p.43 (BR): Douglas Noblet/All Canada Photos/Corbis; p.44: Adam Jones/Visuals Unlimited/Corbis; p.45 (1)T: Julian W/Shutterstock, (2)T: Sandy Hedgepeth/Shutterstock, (3)T: jakit17/Shutterstock, (4)T: Dennis W. Donohue/Shutterstock, (5)T: David Davis/Shutterstock, (C): Kim Taylor/Nature Picture Library/Corbis, (CL): moodboard/Alamy, (CR): Theerapol Pongkangsanan/Shutterstock, (BL): Ziggylives/Shutterstock, (BC): Olha Insight/Shutterstock, (BR): rdonar/Shutterstock; p.46-47: Kristian Buus/Alamy; p.49 (Emily) & (Sophie) & p.50 (CR): Peter Titmuss/Alamy; p.49 (Josh): Stephen Simpson/Getty Images, (Jacob): Juanmonino/Getty Images; p.50 (CL): Judith Collins/Alamy, (BL): Jill Chen/Shutterstock, (b): Gabe Palmer/Alamy, (BR): Shailth/Shutterstock, (TR), (C): Nino Mascardi/Getty; p.53 (B/G): Barry Downard/Getty, (BR): Flip Nicklin/Minden Pictures/Corbis, p.55 (1)T: DYLAN MARTINEZ/Reuters/Corbis, (2)T: Finnbar Webster/Alamy, (3)T: Andrew Wood/Alamy, (4)T: Steve Heap/Shutterstock, (CL): Tetra Images/Alamy; (CR): Celia Peterson/arabianEye/Corbis, (BR): Red Images, LLC/Alamy; p.56 (1): Sabina Jane Blackbird/Alamy, (2): happydancing/Shutterstock, (4): chonrawit boonprakob/Shutterstock, (T): Blend Images/Shutterstock; p.58: Elena Schweitzer/Shutterstock.

Commissioned photography by Gareth Boden: p.11 (TL), (TR); p.13 (project BR); p.17 (1), (2), (3), (4); p.18 (1)T, (2)T; p.21 (TL), (TR); p.23 (project BR); p.28 (TL), (TC), (TR); p.31 (T); p.33 (project BR); p.39; p.43 (TL), (TR); p.45 (project BR); p.50 (T), (CL); p.53 (T); p.55 (project BR).

Workbook
p. 4 (unit header): © TongRo Images/Alamy; p. 5: pirita/Shutterstock; p. 7 (B/G): KPG_Payless/Shutterstock; p. 7 (TR): © Rob Walls/Alamy; p. 10 (unit header): © Martyn Goddard/Alamy; p. 10 (wood frames): homydesign/Shutterstock; p.10 (gold frames): worker/Shutterstock; p. 12 (unit header): © David Wong/Getty; p. 12 (photo 1): Premaphotos/Alamy; (photo 2): Johan Larson/Shutterstock; (photo 3): sevenke/Shutterstock; (photo 4): Roman Sigaev/Shutterstock; (photo 5): Alexander Mak/Shutterstock; (photo 6): E. Spek/Shutterstock; (photo 7): hramovnick/Shutterstock; (photo 8): vaklav/Shutterstock; (photo 9): Perutskyi Petro/Shutterstock; (photo 10): Jaroslav74/Shutterstock; p. 15 (B/G): liubomir/Shutterstock; p. 18 (unit header): Laszio Halasi/Shutterstock; p. 19 (BR): Vetapi/Shutterstock; p. 20 (unit header): © Kike Calvo/National Geographic Society/Corbis; p. 21 (photo 1): Amy Myers/Shutterstock; (photo 2): Monkey Business Images/Shutterstock; (photo 3): © Adrian Sherratt/Alamy; (photo 4): wavebreakmedia/Shutterstock; p. 23 (B/G): Mark Herreid/Shutterstock; p. 25 (photo 1): neelsky/Shutterstock; (photo 2): S-F/Shutterstock; (photo 3): Korionov/Shutterstock; (photo 4): Ti Santi/Shutterstock; (photo 5): Elena Elisseeva/Shutterstock; (photo 6): EBFoto/Shutterstock; (photo 7): TSpider/Shutterstock; (photo 8): dotshock/Shutterstock; (photo 9): stable/Shutterstock; p. 26 (unit header): Lightspring/Shutterstock; p. 27 (BR): Radu Bercan/Shutterstock; p. 29 (TR): Purestock/Alamy; (BR): © Cultura RM/Alamy; p. 30 (unit header): © Randy Plett/Getty; (TR): Joshua Hodge Photography/Getty; p. 32 (TR): © Heide Benser/Corbis; p. 33 (B/G): ThomasLENNE/Shutterstock; p. 36 (unit header): © Adam Jones/Visuals Unlimited/Corbis; p. 37 (TR): Stewart Cohen/Corbis; p. 38 (unit header): © Kristian Buus/Corbis; p. 40: David Ashley/Corbis; p. 41 (B/G): Shailth/Shutterstock; TR: Nino Mascardi/Getty; p. 45 (BR): Mile Atanasov/Shutterstock; p. 46 (TL): Hero Images Inc./Corbis; p. 47 (photo 1): JGI/Jamie Grill/Getty; (photo 2): Offscreen/Shutterstock; (photo 3): Roger Jegg/Shutterstock; (photo 4): D. Pimborough/Shutterstock; (photo 5): © Ian Miles/Flashpoint Pictures/Alamy; (photo 6): © Andrea Heselton/Alamy; (photo 7): tama2012/Shutterstock; (photo 8): © Arcaid Images/Alamy; p. 55 (puzzle header): Stepan Popov/Shutterstock.

Our special thanks to the following for their kind help during location photography:

Barratt Developments PLC; Queen Emma Primary School

Front Cover photo by Sylvestre Machado/Getty Images